THIS BOOK BELONGS TO

Mēgan Kersting

OF SNAILS
AND SKYLARKS

ALSO BY CHRISTY BROWN

My Left Foot
Down All the Days
A Shadow on Summer
Wild Grow the Lilies

POETRY
The Poems of Christy Brown
Background Music

OF
SNAILS
AND
SKYLARKS

Poems by

Christy Brown

STEIN AND DAY/*Publishers*/New York

First published in the United States of America in 1978
Copyright © 1977 by Christy Brown
All rights reserved
Printed in the United States of America
Stein and Day/*Publishers*/Scarborough House,
Briarcliff Manor, N.Y. 10510

Library of Congress Cataloging in Publication Data

Brown, Christy, 1932-
    Of snails and skylarks.

    I. Title.
PR6052.R589403   1978   821'.9'14   78-7619
ISBN 0-8128-2522-5

To the inhabitants of Sweetdom

Contents

OF SNAILS
AND SKYLARKS

Sunset Star

Girl in the wind
blowing wide open
the closed doors of my life –
which way are we going?

Standing against the lurid sky
on the stark brink of ocean
arms outstretched
as if your love and hunger
would embrace the world
and I in my inner room
playing my poetic permutations
can only look and ask the unanswerable.

Brave and cunning I speak to my typewriter
knowing it will not answer back
knowing it will not reply
what I ask and do not want to hear
as you with the vast sunset merge
a multitude of dreams away
uniquely alone and outside of me
in the purity and rarity of this moment
immeasurably beyond my love and my rage

and with the dying call of gulls
the echo resounds:

Girl in the wind
throwing aside
the tight shutters of my life –
which way are we going?

Finding

You touched my flawed body
                        so gently with your eyes
as later with the infinite gentleness
                        of your mind
when the world stopped screaming
                        and turned to the slow rhythm
of our discovered music.

Improbably finding me out
                        in that room reeking of smoke
and mindless bombast
                        as islanded on the fringe of
frantic talk
                        sourly aswim with whisky
lonelier than death
                        and half in love with that grey
inevitability
                        I counted my threadbare bag of pinched
blessings
                        babbling in an idiot cell with no one
to hear my babytalk but myself
                        till you came and sat beside me out of
nowhere
                        utterly without preamble or verbal foreplay
as if only then we had come into existence
                        out of some speechless experience
into where we then found ourselves
                        talking our heads off and I remember
laughing a lot
                        at and beyond ourselves
                        dissecting Mr Joyce with gusto
discussing the myth-making antics of Yeats
                        impetuously scaling his dark tower
and knowing behind the flying words
                        new selves vastly unknown and unmet

before you entered that hellish room
                              on an everlasting instant of wonder.

Voices in a void droning on
                              bottle rotating from hand to flashing
hand
                    the bruised cloistered air throbbing with
the horror of lives spent
                                          before they had begun
till another day new only to us
                              heaved itself over the rooftops
                                    unseen behind moveless
curtains
                                    though we had already left
had already travelled to where nothing could touch us
                        neither malice nor envy of word or eye
nothing concocted of gnarled minds
                              nothing remotely created could touch
us then
                  we a little in fright of what even then we already
knew
                  as the foolish brave unstoppable words poured
from us
                        even in the great and utter silence of our
hearts
                  telling us of the bright thing that had begun.

You touched my flawed life so gently with love
                              burning upward in dark steady flame
burning me, burning me into healing.

W. H. Auden

I came to you tardy and late
as I usually do to the better things in my life:
this hidden singing land I never knew
of eloquent weathers and the many-tongued sea
changing and ever changeless
drawing the moody skies into its mirror
and a true girl to love and steer my star by
at the comic end of it all
making me contemplate eternity
with rather less rash enthusiasm
than in my unspent years of dreaming.

Others kind in their way insisted I read you
as I climbed the slippery ladder out of my cosy accepted mire
and like being pressed with strong medicine I held back
recalcitrant as a surly upstart pup
growling in its soiled lair
snapping at the hands that would feed it.

You were dead before I stumbled upon the life that was in your
poetry
upending your generation and doing needful miracles
on the ones that came limping or thundering after;
dead but you would not lie safely down
and only in the final weeks did I see your face
televised out of human context
alien to that merciless medium
a craggy continent creviced with living
a rubbery sphere indented with tangled latitudes of honest pain
and the healing laughter that lies behind unambiguous suffering
speaking your verse in a tired unlit voice
as if you wanted to close the door and be gone
to where you might at last pin down peace
drink unending wine and converse with friends
till all the sacred cows came home

the ones that you had not so gaily slaughtered
on that mazed journey into truth.

I yet know only half of your mind
half of the world you made uniquely your own
and the other half beckons like an unexplored country
wherein I shall falter often early and late
be confused and befuddled by so many trails
lured by signs that lead apparently into nowhere
save that the nowhere you inhabited teemed with such life
as to leave me panting and many times lost
in my belated crusade to find you.

Love Song

Mary of ever morning light
enter as music into my waking

cover me with your tenderness
from the grey terrors of myself

yours the strength of flowers
rooted in crevices of my heart

out of the wanton wind's way
blossom in my darkness

bringing the laggard world alive
upon your smile and stilling

the night's rage and tumult
in wordless wealth of caring

deep as flowers or love can reach
your daily miracle of healing

Mary of ever morning light
always as music in my waking.

City Airs

When I was yet reaching to be a man
I met a quayside courtesan
with arrogant and immediate eyes
and no time for haggling compromise.

It was high July and in the shade
of the masted ships she plied her trade
and more for pity than quick silver pence
she taught me pain and commonsense.

She looked into my eyes and saw
the lineaments of leafy awe
and with deft sleight of hand and tongue
brought me the terror of being young.

With facile sleight of tongue and hand
she drew maps I did not understand
as the great ships with sails undone
lay festering in the squalid sun.

And in the surly conspiring shade
with lip and tongue and hand she played
hidden symphonies undefined
beyond the slipping grasp of mind.

With windswept hair from scarf unfurled
she held the rash wisdom of the world
taught me man's uniqueness from beast –
for one most singular hour at least.

Along the quays and into the flame
of sunset she went without a name
and my steps are back where it began
and still I reach out to be that man

who when his little hour had burned
got on a bus and never returned.

Act of Contrition

I am sad as the morning begins
for the sudden death of the simple life
I once imagined I was born for
lying deflowered now upon the tatty high altar of ambition
before it had a chance to enjoy its virginity.

Sad too in a remote metaphysical way
for the way things are in China;
reeking with rice and bamboo fervour
all that rice and all that fervour
all that murderous dedication
eternities of patient padded feet marching
pounding out miracles of anonymity
that universal good
choicest ruby in that stark crown
a vast sheet of carbon paper
drawn over the seething land
sucking the soul away.

I am sad for reading that stupid novel last night
wasting the nocturnal virtues of sea-watching
not remembering a single snide simper of it;
sadder still for writing that stupid novel last year
that shrill little Jericho of collapsible walls
throwing stones at myself
a stationary target
and not once hitting the mark;
in extravagant excess of contrition
I am already sorry for the novel I am about to write –
which is being sorry with a vengeance.

Today for want of somewhere else to exile my eyes
I watched the tide come in late
and felt sad for the laggard waves
lurching drunkenly on sharp-tongued rocks

like errant husbands belching home to fuming spouses
sure of a similar scalding;
the amatory cat slinking through the wet grass love-replete
belly touching ground in satiety
a drowned item the sea had disgorged
in disgust at its own gluttony.

Up in the dark saturnine Northland
studded with silent singsong lakes
and hills loud with dead men's tales
where once I heaped lavish untrue praises
upon a long-legged woman and lusted for her out of reason
until I put aside that curious little day
somebody is already being shot
for Christ and country
blood reddening the heather or pavement
the orange or green bullet
fired by us all awake or asleep
startling a leaf or window-latch with its report.

Most of all it saddens me to sit here
mooning like a calf besotted with afterbirth
and the abrupt dark draping the sky
writing lines like these so eminently qualified
to be contrite about.

Of Snails and Skylarks

He can tell the colours of the four winds
blowing over the rumpled rainbow land

pluck any miracle in or out of season
from out his patchwork bag of magic

slung over his starward-leaning shoulder
mad eyes playing tunes of enchantment

upon rock and leaf and curling grass
telling in the sere hedges of October

a thousand tangled themes and quirky tales
of canny snails and skylarks

He shakes the torpid earth awake
makes it throb beneath his hobnailed music

the smallest stream runs madcap at the sun
and fishes in tremulous depths conspire

to deliver up their sleek cunning
into his green-thumbed keeping

He holds converse with flowering stones
opening beneath his caressing feet

feasts upon bright philosophies of air
and leaving wraps his heart in a cloud

watches it smiling as it floats away
touching steeples as it goes

then laying aside his miracles and music
all wonder accomplished for another day

he forsakes the world of snails and skylarks
and steps sadly down into the harlot streets

that spawned and still sternly spurn him
hiding in his heart a smuggled fugitive joy

lighting the broad wasted dark of that meaner time.

Now and Not Then

Shall the dire day break when life
finds us merely husband and wife
with passion not so much denied
as neatly laundered and put aside
and the old joyous insistence
trimmed to placid coexistence?

Shall we sometime arise from bed
with not a carnal thought in our head
look at each other without surprise
out of wide awake uncandid eyes
touch and know no immediate urge
where all mysteries converge?

Speak for the sake of something to say
and now and then put on a display
of elaborate mimicry of the past to prove
that ritual reigns where once ruled love
and calmly observe those bleak rites
that once made splendour of our nights?

Dear, when we stop being outrageous
and no longer find contagious
the innumerable ecstasies we find
in rise of hand or leap of mind –
not now or then, love, need we fear thus;
those two sad people will not be *us*.

In Memory of Melba
Our Cat

You did not long enjoy
the unexplored wonders of this other Eden
you of the purring yellow-eyed persuasion
skipping in and so abruptly out of our lives
running rashly off into feline eternity
under the bouncing wheels of a country trailer.

No more than a kitten yourself, girl,
and we who had fumed at your early courting
are thankful now that you gave us as parting gift
three carbon copies of yourself as souvenirs
to help heal the wound of your passing
in a purring concourse of caring.

No more will you wake me from futile dreaming
your velvet presence padding over my face
miaowing me back to bleary-eyed reality
wanting not my meagre comfort
but to share your warmth with me
out of the sleek largesse of your nature.

The sea will be melancholy for a while
with you not there to distract me
from the due contemplation of beauty
by insisting that I look first upon your own
and for the first time in many weeks
the morning ashes will be undisturbed in the grate.

The new home that you had just begun to rule
will be loud now with your sudden absence
until the three gentle reminders you bequeathed us
begin slowly to fill the furry void.

Pique

My wife, otherwise an agreeable perspicacious helpmate,
has one pernicious failing:
she reads other writers.
A blatant act of infidelity
short of the other easier variety
which I could take in my stride
with a large pinch of arsenic.

She not merely reads other writers
but has the nerve to enjoy them
dissecting their outpourings
with critical élan
taking them to bed with her every night.
Not quite what the wife of a writer
ought really to do
when all is unsaid and undone
sending me into murky fits
of quite juvenile pique
as I take it out on my typewriter
belting it until its innards groan
banging my head against the invisible wall
of her insatiable booklore.

She spends hours away from me
locked in somebody else's world
embroiled in some other bloody writer's fantasies
quite ignoring the ones that are spinning round in my head
and despoiling innocent sheets of paper
as I eject them forth like spittle
not having anything better to do
between the cup and the leering lip.

A novel in her immaculate hands
becomes a desert between us
while I sourly contemplate

the alphabet on my keyboard
as between the literary covers she snuggles
shameless as sharing another bloke's bed.

What spectacle could be worse
than glowering impotent on the sidelines
while my wife devours with unappetised abandon
other traders of the word incarnate?

The Poetry Reading

Trapped and beleaguered in a web of guests
garrulous unto the perilous point of endurance
set upon ushering in the new day
with last-gasp wheezing of applause
we looked at each other
across the littered chasm of mashed cigarettes
and tumblers aswirl with debris of slaughtered drinks
looking for hopeful signs of departure
and as before found only gaping mouths
insatiable and unstoppable
opening on profligate inanities
bruising the reeking walls with ballads
patriotic paeans extolling the mercifully dead
roaring the praises of nubile native daughters
long removed from lascivious gaze
beguiling the worms with their mythic charms;
knee-thumping fists flailing in lickspittle emphasis
beating out our limp-lidded doom
sending the spectre of sleep scurrying
over the ink-black night bay
as gallant and gracious to the bilious end
we smiled and politely nodded and blinked our eyes
skewered to the convivial stake of friendship
hope of repose long kicked into exile
pacing the desolate hills
as the unending carousel continued
caught in a time-trap of bonhomie.

I slipped into threadbare refuge of apathy
listening with marginal focus of attention
as the court jester beside me told a joke
done to haggard death all evening
concerning a rural chiropodist
who, when asked to lend a hand to a stranded pub-bound
    motorist,
could only proffer a foot . . .

Out of fierce self-willed torpor I awoke
to see a small miracle taking place;
holding the slim volume of my poems in your hands
as if holding a fiery Book of Job
in an attitude of implacable Thespian command
you were declaiming forth my pallid verses
in your best Bernhardt tones of faith
a deft Delphic nymph of sleeklimbed bombast
throwing pearls of imperishable truth and profundity
upon the slack-jawed philistines gathered at your feet
a receding sea of stunned befuddled faces
whisky hands stayed stupefied in mid-air
by this silk-and-steel siren of Poesy majestic in their midst
making each of them in quick turn suddenly homesick
and hastening en masse to quit the holy temple . . .

Alone at last we smiled
and raised a final glass in tired triumph and homage
to that slender sesame of our deliverance
you still held like a scimitar in your hands
as the waves broke and brightened below us
and waking birds shook the grey hedges into life.

Victoria

From this unimagined pinnacle of my new life
every gentle now and then you come back
out of a past neither of us ever really knew
still less apprehended with total mind
save as sometimes we remember music
heard only in dream
and all the more real for that
touching chords buried beyond words to capture
beyond life's sad erosions.

I made for you once a small poem
born out of a comic cameo you had painted
of you working minor kinetic miracles
at some crazy pre-dawn California carnival
wherein I begged you not to look
too closely into my shopsoiled soul
and in mercy turn aside those merciless lenses
for fear you would finally discover me;
thankfully you looked the kinder way
sparing me at least that truth
that so graced your letters.

Your name fell exotic on my senses
hardened to plainer greyer sounds
and I recall how at last
after talkative eons of pages
had traversed the ocean between us
you brought to the surface of our dialogue
the particular pigmentation of your skin
long before the paltry pundits of popular idiom
had ever linked black with beautiful;
in turn you knew well enough by then
the many-weathered colours of my mind
to wonder about the hue of my skin.

You scared and shamed me with your young intensity
angry with the collective stupidities of humankind
making my zealous apathy a tawdry fake
my well-tended sophisticated boredom with life
a hollow laugh in an empty banquet hall
my heart a vessel looted of compassion.

Yesterday was something we savoured
with our finer perceptions
with keener felicities of sense
than are likely to attend us ever afterwards;
with the unreturnable rhythm of the sea
impassable and wide as destiny
yesterday ebbed away
found refuge on another safer shore
leaving fragile imprints
we shall trace in our minds forever.

Beached now under my singular star
lighting me into new understanding and love
you shine on the soft pure rim of that world
and enter ever gentle now and then
with gifts of simple peace and charity in your hands

making the broad spaces between us
flower with meaning.

Vamp

All jaded airs and faded graces
out of daylong hibernation you emerge
to saunter down the main street swivel-hipped
high heels clacking on cobblestones
beating out a staccato come-hither beat
mascaraed eyes alert for evening commerce
lashes dark and lustrous and not your own
lacquered hair piled in perilous pyramids
some incautious chap might in a soft moment touch
and pull fingers away stung as from barbed wire.

You are an anachronism and you know it
had you words to frame the thought
but are too tired to care
for the need that drives you down such mean ways
is never outdated.

Men with hunted rabbit faces
married past recollection of slighter freedoms
teetering with sick qualms into tepid middleage
ogle you in the gloom of the lounge bar
their brood hens of wives sipping gin and tonic
moistily enmeshed in home truths and grandchildren
and the automatic smile of response
cracking your rouged and powdered cheek
flutters a moment in the musty air
and falls to grief into the deep-pile carpet
midway between you and those stout agricultural wallets
stricken across a minefield of grassy boots
and sodden cigarette ends

and the faint Lotharios turn aside
smirking into their pints
settling for domestic twilight
and the naggin home in the hip pocket.

And nobody sees you home save the stars
and the mangy mongrel yapping at your ankles
frantic for want of a kind slurred word
out of your twisted red mouth.

Cursing you lunge into the wailing night
raw brambles tugging at your ancient fur jacket
lifting the jarring latch on your door
kicking out the world of tight pockets
and tighter mercies.

To the flickering grate you stumble
numbed hands outstretched
to catch the last of the heat
from the embers of the only fire left.

Lonely Madrigal

London flounders in my Lady's golden wake.

In this crabbed hour of lonely themes
cracked lads and freckled lasses of my stripling years
come crowding back to cloud the dusty mirror of memory
stirring dulled images of vanquished vanities
as that fabulous bringer of my latecoming joy
once more claims London as her own
and gathers it into her scented palm.

Risen from playful dust they return
to taunt my jaded genes with remembered verve
laughing dare-devil lads and scornful sun-licked girls
as stooped and bent with loss
I crouch above my typewriter
dredging murky depths for words to drown the image
of the morning star of my querulous middle-years
dangling London on the pellucid tips of her fingers.

In puny rage I populate this tumultuous silence
with hoarse affirmations of self-sufficiency
battling with elements attuned to inner mayhem
carving upon the rude rock of time a brief postscript
of diminishing pith and traitor wisdom
borrowed from sources I no longer have right or light to enter
and only this patient beast of purring metal answers back
shuddering under my insane bellowings
as scoundrel London swivels and rotates
upon a turn of my Lady's impeccable wrist.

I claw out hidden hieroglyphics of meaning
in the threatening swarm of this early dark
creeping like ink across the unquiet bay
touching my mind with dire intimations of coming terrors

and the shawl of rough desperate logic I wrap round me
grows hourly more threadbare
admitting the dreaded draught of her intolerable absence
who quenches the lurid lamps of London in her look.

I huddle in the hollow rock of no solace
seeking refuge in past pretensions of peace
turning over random stones of once radiant hue
and finding underneath the utter blight of promise
filling with decay of unfound purpose this soulless room
left a graveyard rank and desecrated
as the torpid pulse of London quickens to her merest gesture.

O London I damn and excoriate you
and call down upon you a thousand plagues
as you flounder in my Lady's golden wake.

Over The Sea to Leeds

Kindly I told myself – a guest in your midst –
that you were in a state of transition
between falling down and standing up
as my friends introduced me to you
on that early morning tour
a hurried get-together I grant you
and from my high perch
eagle-eyed on the seat of the van
the local vista was restricted

yet charity has its bounds
eyes were after all made to see
and sadly I saw you at your Sunday worst
making that first dismal morning after disembarkation
more of a grey burden with your encrusted scabs
and open weeping sores oozing urban putrefaction
mocking the far green magic of the hills
receding like a distant dream of Summer away from you
your chimneys scumming the skies

dowager buildings of once civic bloom
huddled together like battered old ladies
in dingy defeated camaraderie
children flitting like lively lice
through the scalded maze of your streets
Sabbatical factory smoke drawing a murky shawl
over your pockmarked pools of desolation
your awful incongruity uncharmed by age
untouched by faint stirrings of a former grace.

I beheld you thus exposed in all your shabby lineaments
and to my utmost chagrin felt tortuously at home.

Broken Rhythm

There I was
grunting in the grey wizened morning
crouched on the hard functional lavatory pot
straining valiantly to do nature's business
and making heavy weather of it
aspiring to put my mind onto higher things
in that cramped smelly fly-besotted cubicle

when over the saloon-like swinging halfdoor
like a bulbous red moon over a hedge
rose a round capped countryman's face
honest in its perplexity and concern
puckered up with childlike curiosity
wanting to know if I needed – of all things – a hand.

For a moment I was angry
at this bovine intrusion
into what was after all an intensely private affair
between my gaseous intractable innards and myself
but soon my unfriendly resentment gave way
to humorous resignation
thinking how absurd our strident insistence upon privacy
in this turgid chamberpot-flush of a life

for at least the face mooning over the halfdoor
was unblemished with mockery
full of brotherly care at my comical plight
though it played bloody havoc with my rhythm.

Terminal Thoughts

Death bores the life out of me.

It no longer intrigues or invites speculation.
It happens so often it has become monotonous.
It is an overplayed exercise in melancholy
akin to sex in its inflated reputation.

What offends me most about death
is its abject lack of imagination.
As often as not it is a dull business
denying that sense of theatre
immured in the dullest soul
seldom nudging us over into fantasy.

We seldom get the death we deserve.
As in life second-best is the reigning norm.
The vast grey majority of men and women
die deaths of unsurpassed mediocrity
bathed in a thin aura of pointless poignancy
giving us slight pause in our crowded trivia
to make clichéd comment upon the piquancy of the end.

In our urgency to liven it up a bit
we invest death with an inventive streak
it does not remotely begin to possess
except of course when it happens to us.
Then it is a sad and magnificent thing
compelling the respect and compassion of all who gaze upon it.
Then for the first time in our lives perhaps we hold the stage
and nothing is going to cheat us of the limelight
least of all the mundane act of dying.

Death is so often a distinct non-event.
Even the most incandescent of lives

can be ruined by a wretched curtain
falling halfway between a belch and a sigh.
And princes too once bluff and portly as Hal
of far-famed bestialities and resplendent lusts
seldom thunder topheavy into laughing graves
but choke to death of obese surfeit on a mouldy wine cork
and slide into ponderous boxes wormy with weariness
or lacking even that last lachrymose grace
linger like chilled refugees in the bleak deserted foyer
long after their insipid little drama is over
to splutter into infantile incoherence
on soggy sodden gobbets of gutless bravado
stuck in their wasted gullets.

Death and dignity seldom see eye to eye.
The best way to die is to be alive while you are doing it
with all five senses and others in full flight
in full-throated green-gold career
before the final obscenity of linen sheets
that unnatural landscape of dim candles and muted voices
and gloved hands pressing forth in observed ritual grief
lest we awaken in another time and overhear
these pallid lamentations hurting our repose
and weep for having once been alive.

Friend, you are more than welcome to death;
it is something I can well do without.

Lapwing

Lapwing alighting
bringing the morning alive
setting the sad sea in motion
putting the tardy sun in its place

making the grass leap before our eyes
dipping gracefully into our lives
taking earth and sky under wing
a quiver of sleek pride

then into the morning with you.

A Kind of Prayer

Call me, Lord, as call You must
in the carnival midst of my sins
for surely that is where it all begins
at last to make sense of this foolish dust
when the all too escapable charms
and infidel conspiring alarms
that hold us tightly in thrall
as we precariously crawl
about our little plot
loosen and lamely fall
from our inhospitable skins
and nothing more we crave
of sunset or dawn
prizes lost or newly won
or tenacious images haul
from our initial nowhere
above or below the indifferent air
within or beyond the garrulous grave
our brief bolt shot
with no need then to act brave
or lament our gaudy lot
and we no longer there.

Call me, Lord, as call You will
in the dawn or dusk of sinning
while I still dream of winning
one more rowdy hour to fill
my mouth full of the usual stuff
of nonsense and whisky in measure enough
to buoy me through another day
content to let the devil pay
my eyes peeled for sudden wonders
on every random breeze
still capable of self-surprise
and unwarrantable surmise

still adept at making blunders
in traversing the thin trapeze
above the torn nets of sanity
the waiting pitfalls of inanity
O I'd rather go while I am ahead
before having to pay the inevitable toll
with my inconsequential soul
against all debts accumulated
as I dawdled and procrastinated
in earning my daily bread –
bad enough at any time to be dead
without going on the immortal dole.

Come get me, Lord, awake or asleep
in prancing April or sad-eyed October
wild in my cups or ponderously sober
and if that most singular girl should weep
at whose footfall my aspirations leap
give her all the comfort You can
with promise of a happier plan
just waiting around the next bend –
let her know my passing isn't the end
of all brighter things to come to her
that light and music can still occur
with me no longer hanging around
to mutter a single possessive sound.

Come swift or slow, Lord, loud or soft
under swoon of moon or glare of day
with my crazed senses with me or away
bearing me downward or aloft
as long as You come where my story begins
in the merciful heyday midst of my sins.

John Millington Synge

Uncouth as the wind
rising out of mist and fire
you heeded as the sea told tales
and yielded up to you its passionate lore.

Transfixed by rainbows you stood
by the gaping wounds of the smitten land
and emptied your painful soft-vowelled love
into its bitter dreaming brood.

Let wiser minds than I possess
grant or deny your place as seer and singer
of blood themes more wildly imagined
and still more savagely lived
now passed from the tongues of men
beyond pale logic to discover or dissect
for having once lived in or out of time
beauty lives forever shadowed in its own radiance.

I only know you brought the roar of Aran waves
crashing in angry splendour upon my stony threshold
and caused the walls of my bleak solitary room
to blaze brightly once with heather and thistledown

hurting my city-snared eyes
and troubling my heart out of muteness
until sparrow and skylark were one
bearing the rooftops away.

Lost Item

The man was crying
                    as no child could ever cry
hard bitter wailing
                    unforced as raw act of nature
shaking his birdcage chest
                    draped in ignominious hospital pyjamas
stooped in wan morning light by high-barred window
                    vein-curdled hands clasped
rigid as taut-strung wire
                    tonsured head bowed in bereavement
as the day rattled and clattered
                    cups passed around
swimming with tepid tea.

Male nurses in brisk no-nonsense white uniforms
                    whom I had maligned as "deflowered eunuchs"
the night of my admittance
                    twisting in whisky fulminations
were ordinary blokes again doing a job
                    shaking out night-rumpled sheets
turning man-soiled mattresses
                    spoon-feeding infirm tremulous men
whose ages could no longer be deciphered
                    lost in rambling mazes of oblivion
swift adept young hands wiping dribbling drooling mouths
                    tender as any woman and companionable
exchanging ribald anecdotes of nights off
                    whistling the latest pop tunes
taking no notice whatever
                    of the weeping man.

Red-eyed and hating the world
                    I peered over the rough rim of my blanket
wincing at the din of delf
                    the clang and canker of morning

creeping out of my bestiary of bludgeoned pleasures

               beholding the man then crying in light
amazed by such unchecked male grief

               wondering how these cheery young men
uniformed in the business of healing

               could bear to pass him by unheeding
standing by the cell-like window

               blighted by some unnameable loss
tears making mockery of his harpooned manhood

               swaying barefoot on cold boards
a thin blue-striped totem pole

               uprooted and left to brutish elements
riven down his scarecrow lacerated length.

Unable further to stand the spectacle

               easily outraged by bland faces
passing unobservant and incurious all about

               in loud hearty ups-a-daisy bonhomie
I demanded a key to this sorrowful mystery in our midst

               and was informed by a brash young scallion
of under twenty amid a white welter of teeth:
"Michael Joe, is it?

               Oh, he's a bit upset
because he can't remember where

               he left his fuckin' dentures last night –"
He paused square hand assured in mid-air

               and smiled winningly down –
"It *is* two spoonfuls, isn't it?"

Cobra

Habit
coiling uncoiling
cobra in grass
strangling strong and delicate
strands of ancient affinities
poison drawing poison
minus hope of antidote
save the slippery slide
home into oblivion
the dying unending
and that too an illusion
windowless reality
mirroring always
the threat of tomorrow
deadlier than bite of now
oozing into pores
liquefied terror
slithering
cobra in grass.

Antiseptic den
of shambling shadow men
coughing up life
uniformed in despair
chained ankles rubbing
the cobra waits
coils uncoils
moves slow
slinky with intent
forking fangs
into sodden minds
soft as rotten fruit
gargoyle charade
brainless unison
invisibly fettered

life once shared
once consummated
shredded
sick moist joke
dribbling into apathy
slackjawed
in the final reel.

Habit
viperish wise
slicing
through caring
killing roots
no more indomitable
once strong
as love called home
redemption
cold echo
in wilderness
little shambling mice-men
twittering in a cage
biting
the quick of their lives
in swift savage snaps
gleeful in dying.

Habit
is what I wear now
snug as the last shroud.

Morning Glory

Above the morning waves I behold
in a tumble of brown and gold
my Venus rising from the sea –
albeit somewhat listlessly.

The enchantment of the waking shore
cannot quite banish the night before
as with hair in glorious disarray
she stumbles forth to greet the day.

Over the coffee and untouched toast
I see traces of last night's ghost
lurking in those fabulous eyes
unwilling to meet the breaking skies.

Lo, the sun ignites her hair, and she
turns that radiant look on me
and with breathless intonations
murmurs of perilous palpitations.

Light and delight of eye and limb
moving as one inspiring hymn
weaving with lithe deliberate tread
her precarious way back to bed.

Leaving me to contemplate
in my own somewhat unsteady state
how even Beauty of such queenly shine
cannot quite outwit a little wine.

Dear Dilemma

This is surely the ultimate catalyst –
you are off to see your analyst.

The ageless story reads so well –
less now of heaven and more of hell;
you no longer derive stimulation
from my brilliant conversation;
as I pulsate with volcanic desire
you sit reading novels by the fire
your mind elsewhere to strangers grown
and not one of the bloody novels my own;
not only do you shun my perennial company –
you don't even glance now at my latest poetry
a fate that is infinitely worse than death
for one who spews verse with every breath.

Where once my witticisms would have scored
now they merely make you bored
and those outpourings you once deemed lyrical
now only render you slightly hysterical
for try as you might you cannot disguise
the desperation in your eyes
the peculiar way you hold the breadknife
while I babble on about the sanctity of life
as from heights we once considered exotic
I bring you down to the merely neurotic.

Most evenings now we sit glassy-eyed
every small tension magnified
warding off mutual scorn and derision
staring blind and mute at television
all past delights gone sour and cloyed
as you get ready at length to meet your new-found Freud
leaving me alone to wince and contemplate
the bare brittle bones of our marital state

neither lovable clown nor nimble sage
sinking too soon into bilious middleage.

You married me for better or for worse –
but you reckoned without my atrocious verse
or the times I would limp from my mental hovel
to have another tired go at that damn novel
the English of Avon's Swan to bludgeon
with apoplectic flights of pith and high dudgeon
hammerstrokes of bucolic grit and wrath
slithering down the traitorous path
of inordinate imagined wrongs and indignation
with notions immeasurably above my station
which far from making you proud or elated
made you gradually quite sedated.

And in your eyes there sometimes hovers
shades of past innumerable lovers
who would grovel for your merest touch
and count themselves blessed if you as much
as brushed their hapless brows with your lips
sending them spinning over into total eclipse
hastening to your every beck and call
poor slaves and besotted servants all
cast aside desolate and discarded
disconsolate and broken-hearted
floundering in your starry wake
all for my bombastic sake.

And this is the melancholy final twist
beyond cure by faith quack or psychiatrist;
hellfire in my breast will continue to rankle
as my life story twines around your delectable ankle.

Dolphins

Out of dreamy early morning eyes we saw them
rising upon the languid incoming waves
disporting themselves with impish grace in the sun
as if gliding that bright moment out of fantasy
solely for our shared unutterable delight.

Pearly portents of promise in the infant day
forging a private ballet for our waking eyes
indifferent to our silent applause
giving us brief entrance
to their lucid universe.

Making us pause to marvel at the music
in slow stir of surf and sigh of leaf
lending to our minds gentle assurance
of sharing with these shining friends
our little clifftop eyrie of heartsong.

In the instant it took our entranced eyes
to lift and find each other again
they had gone back into fantasy
lest we suffer by our gazing
too great a surfeit of joy.

They danced upon the waves long afterwards
a wineglow upon our gladdened senses.

A Song For My Body

What quite undivine act of comedy
landed us together in the same suit of skin?
Welded as one in this ungainly unholy alliance
so often with damn all to say to each other
communications awry and in a tangled mess
of jangled nerve-endings that never end
transmitting like drunken telephonists
bawling out contradictions in beleaguered defiance
wading through a morass of perennial cross-purposes
screaming frenzied morse code signals
when there is no marrow of meaning in the messages?

Sing a song of no pence
retrogressive nonsense;
what sort of clown is at the helm
of our incongruous realm?

Thrown into this crazy unending waltz
without preamble or introduction
without being asked if we even liked one another
we trip each other up at every hazardous step
stumbling over cunningly concealed obstacles
locked in a sweaty unwelcome embrace
in a twist of unaesthetic turbulence
in a murderous shadow-game of coexistence.

A rare time the miracle happens;
freedom's bright brief shaft falls between us
as out of orbit we dance in our separate spheres
only to collide once more in explosive conjunction
come as ever too soon upon the old weary reckoning
and crawl again inside the same hateful habitation
skulking and seething in our mutual loathing.

Sing a song of no hope
for poor derided joe soap;
what mocking hand pulls the string
of our inelegant capering?

In the narrowness of your lean miserly means
I splutter like a guttered candle
taunted by the tantrums of your absurd cravings
your flashing prima donna swoops of need
the gold and grey of your solitudes and solstices
as groaning you heave yourself over the brow of another day
the hard hours contracting to points of no meaning
as you square up to them with tired tinselled bravado
peering through the faded plumage of your dusty decades
and even as I call to you in baffled tenderness
and fury in the ceaseless fray
you lag forever a million heavy years behind.

Sing a song of alien rye
to hell with the wherefore and the why;
what master magician all logic defying
 oins us in this long lugubrious dying?

And still there was a summer . . .
the hot easy contempt of a greener time
stretched at weary length into disgruntled afternoon compromise
after many a false clarion call of passion and alarm
when the blood bounded between us like a sea in torment
love came for the once and only time and made you eloquent
made you almost unique and beautiful
unafraid to acknowledge the presence of mirrors in the world
made of our mutual cell a strange sanctuary
made you weep for the new singing that was in you.

Sing a song of hands and feet
see how the bruised lovers bleat;
what supreme satirist calls the tune
and hails us home from the fair too soon?

When we have been served the last taste of living
and the landlord bellows Time for the last time
I hope we can be gentlemen, you and I, and quietly take our
     leave
with no hangdog regrets or malingering back after hours
when there is nothing left in the bottle but the dregs of yesterday
and you slip into the final folly of the grave
bones and sinews no longer at the beck of random voices
your empty passages strumming with industrious worms
and that daft bewildered battery-box of a brain
all loose screws and twisted wires brittle like wintry twigs
settles into its unfamiliar quietude –

We face another puzzle:

When the crying's over and the quick tears dry –
who will have the last laugh, you or I?

Memo to a Fellow Sufferer

Where do you ride tonight, brother bard,
upon the range under the stars?
Chatting up the mots of Madrid
bedazzling the birds of Barcelona
with that liquorice tongue of yours
meddling with their mantillas
under dark Moorish walls
so many alien Mollies blooming
where the sperm flows as fast as the brandy?

Do you perchance sit and sup
with fanatic thin-lipped jesuits
plotting the come-uppance of the state
your full May moon face shining
with prospects of arcane anarchy?
Still persecuted by Liffey nightmares
still fat and foolish as a fox on booze and bombast?
In your sensuous siestas do you sometimes catch
the slap of Arklow waves turgid
against barnacle-thick painted hulls?
Above the roar of the bullfight
the dying bellow of the bull
do you sometimes hear the far screech of Moore Street
the beloved fishwives of fable belting your ears?

You're not missing much
so slay the illusion of nostalgia
before it gets you in its tentacles again.

The Hail Marys are thick in Dublin tonight
and there's another bloody penny on the pint.

Nocturnal

Across the sleeping bay
a yellow moon plays havoc
with the cloudy continents
throwing a truculent charm
over shape and form and shadow
alive in coiled suspension
piercing the smooth thin shell
trapping capricious thought.

Symphonic waves below
shed dark pulses of peace
on the craggy foreshore
stark fingers reaching
in arrogant moonlight
hurting with jagged hints
of simple witchcraft
creeping about the murmuring room.

Gradual joy breaks
surging upon slow waves
glints of bruised brilliance
breaking upon brittle barriers
routing tired old suspicions
a silver shoal to read magic by
and lost shipwrecked things.

Faces from another time
articulate with love
rise between the moon and tears
unbidden from a buried somewhere
blind the white world of sea and cloud
for a long glimmering moment.

The Dunce

I could certainly live without you if I tried;
it is the trying that is so unthinkable.

I could learn to live alone with myself again
if I was not such a poor scholar at learning
that kind of intricate monumental lesson
and be able to go back into the cave again
and find my steps in the once familiar dark.

I could, for instance, watch a sunset without you,
hear birds without wishing to share their song with you,
listen to Mahler or Sibelius of a single evening
and not rage to have you in the same room.

The sea would surely speak the same things to my mind
and deliver up its immemorial magic as ever
with you not there to decipher it for me
with magic the sea could never own.

In your absence I might even write a love poem
and afterwards read it to the listening night
without choking to death on the mangled words
and losing all sense in the grief of your going.

I could find my way into books again without you
maybe into the writing of books without you
and not know the terrifying panic and sweat
of showing you what I have written.

I could begin to understand the hieroglyphics of my life
without you there to decode each symbol for me;
the little mysteries might unravel themselves
without your tender tutelage to prepare me.

Learning to live without you would be rather like
learning to die each moment I drew breath
and if that is the most vital lesson I can learn
let me remain a dunce the rest of my days.

Moon Ruse

They were lovers
of an ordinary stamp
and did not see flowers
other than things in a field
heard music as pleasant sounds
coming out of instruments
holding no ecstatic terrors
bringing no holy unease
to their mild middling minds
and when they held hands
no fire flashed between them
no symphony of panic swelled
crashing as the sea in giant need
and they looked at each other kindly
without being thunderstruck
the blood in their veins easeful as pipesmoke
and found life good.

Until the conjuring moon
one night told them lies
weaved fantasies of unbelief
till flowers were fables of glory
music a torrent in the air
rending the clouds with fire
the very stones underfoot
high altars of desire unfathomed
leading into abysses of surpassing joy
hung jewel-like upon their fingertips
the blood in their veins raging as Lucifer
calling up fiery kingdoms of sense
drowning in swoons of discovery
making life a livid word made flesh.

In the morning mild and married
they ask politely did the other sleep well

pass the marmalade and milk
spoon their tea dreamily
and contemplate the potted plants
lying on the windowsill
before the clock tells them
they are once more released
into their separate day.

The moon merely informs them now it is time for bed.

Remembering A Friend:
Robert Collis

The horse came back alone
over the morning hills of Wicklow
no longer bearing its master .
missing the gentle guidance of your hand
nudging it into homecoming
mistily wondering perhaps
why you had stayed behind
why you had fallen
so soft and sudden
to earth
wordless in the wet grass
a moment ago you had ridden over like the wind
surveying your green valley as ever with love.

Down that smoking air a lone calling
hushing your high heart in a cloud
bearing you away from the valley and the city
from tenements darkly swarming with stunted life
and sibilant streams and hedges brimming with song
you knew and celebrated with conjoined agony and affection
that sudden swift whisper on the wind
in one swallow rush of zealous possession
stealing your breath past stream and pavement
in that moment out of time
that finds each of us small and alone
though wind and rain and growing things of earth
were brothers to you in that last union
and sang you proud into peace
under a turbulent sky
where your heart's abiding passion lay.

You strode rather than stepped through life
crushing many a demure bloom in your career

yet with the blunt sensitivity of one
trading not with images but imperatives
you were solicitous of mute mayhem
crashing through lives indignant with healing
the arrows of your anger flashing into minds
cramped and closeted in grey contumely of office
physician to the anonymous poor and maimed
loud with tenderness for broken things
making strength and basilicas of belief
out of the deep unsaid sorrows of your life
vain and strong and innocent of malice
and beautiful in the last and only sense.

Friend of all my life
seer of my sapling years
I do not feel your absence as pain
for knowledge of love once gained and given
is never lost or betrayed into unknowing
and there are always rainbows.

Men At Work

They loomed out of a grey nowhere
monkey-jacketed against the wind and sly rain
leaning on their trusty shovels chewing philosophies
cupping gutted cigarettes in knuckly fists
no doubt weighing things of high import
between their leather boots and the hanging skies
making the highways safe for cosseted citizens like us
passing by cocooned in cushiony warmth
while they the warrior workers
stood stoic sentinel
spades at the ready
opening up the country for commerce.

At our approach they became workmen once more
making heroic stabs at the wet unyielding tarmac
digging diligently into the hard business of the day
making ingenious little holes in the road
fussy as old maids at pastry
watching us out of hooded wary eyes
as we sped on through the mud
leaving them in the mist
to their butt-ends and craggy ponderings.

We thought it no small deed in our honour
that they had enterprise enough
to at least fake industry
stirred by flurries of decent guilt
while in paper-barricaded citadels across the land
the sleeping masters of the stately ship
stretched dishonourable limbs
and whistled in their subsidised slumbers
waking up between snore and avaricious fantasies
to exhort the populace anew
to greater frenzies of sacrifice
and national fervour.

A Handful of Haiku

1   *Dylan Thomas*
         Out of dawn raging
                in shoals of fire by the sea
       and bile-green bottles.

2   *Jonathan Swift*
         The demented dean
                stabs his quick quill on parchment
       to Vanessa's heart.

3   *Polonius*
         Behind an arras
                dispatched with a Danish thrust
       a paternal spy.

4   *Quasimodo*
         A lump of foolish flesh
            slobbering forth your rage and
                fiercer farce of love.

5   *Sean*
         Ambition unlit
                poor as Christ in Bayswater
       your heart's your coffer.

6   *Dubliner*
         Raw rock-blasting voice
            anointed with Liffey dew
       woos a Spanish maid.

7   *At Two Years Old*
         My nephew runs in
            despoils my easel gaily
                puts Pablo to shame.

8   *That Cat*
         Yellow evil-eyed
              purrs through my leonine wrath
                        and licks my distaste.

Back At Base

The bruised air roars.

I know somewhere out there
beyond the dense green curtains
there is quietness and pause
the beginnings of peace perhaps
in some little back pocket of this city
unmolested by restless minds
attuned to the bedlam
the ceaseless furore
the merciless mass of mechanised living;
but the illusion escapes me now.

Once in the midst of chaos
this moment almost beyond recollection
I could imagine peace
could conjure up images of tranquillity
in the lift and closing of an eyelid
and make it last long enough to forge a dream.

Now only the noise exists
only that is real
where once I bled life
and imagined all my weathers to be.

My nerve-ends terminate here
are beaten into atrophy
bludgeoned to stupefied abstraction.
Not even in fractured sleep
can I grasp the torn threads
leading back into illusion.

Who is dead –
this city or I?

Whose is the corpse I see before me
stretched rigid in the comic contours of death –
my own or those streets that once rejoiced
in the dark and pearly time of my ascending hours?

The answer is not here
but elsewhere in a maze beyond unravelling.

I will come back to this place
again and ever again
and not ever find it again
for not even as a ghost am I at one with it.

Where once song sprang out of cement
and birds regal in stone
now only cement remains
and it no longer speaks bright talk to my mind.

Unearned Income

I have wrestled with death
of a kind
fought the dreary fight
a solo for two voices
in a minor key
one strident with fishwife imperatives
my own a slurred belch
heaved upon a mountain of monotony
upon which I have built my temple
squarely in quicksand.

A jejune joust with death
a tame contest
the outcome assured
in an arena swarming with dusty echoes
and still more dusty choices
in undistinguished darkness
with nothing solid underfoot
nothing palpable to assail
rend apart with absence of logic
hammer into shapelessness.
A boring battle of dull intent
without spectators
without clamour
utterly without glory
the bronzed bedlam of trumpets
no lurid thirst after victory
nor the greater lust after defeat
holding only at its nerveless core
a tepid scepticism
cancelling out belief
in one's instinct to survive
rendering the gilt-edged triumph
of the ageless adversary
a timeless static mockery
trapped in cold laughter.

So have I succeeded
in the crooked middleways of my fourth decade
to this score of unearned income
of sour sedentary wisdom
curled in upon itself
suckled on morbidity
limply taking my own pulse
noting its nonrate
zooming to cosmic zeros of indifference
as the sun climbs bravely out of torpor
to begin another round of weary salutation
on limbs vilely sprawled in acquiescence
and eyelids fast shut against intrusions of joy.

If such be the sum of worldly wisdom
life is then an impoverished joke
and death too great an anti-climax
to warrant serious attention
a hesitant kick in the teeth
where there are only soft gums left.

Beloved Myth

Behold the staunch suburban poet –
though his lines don't always show it –
enduring with grim-jawed tenacity
the trials of his trim-lawned Gethsemane
the heartscald of that promiscuous jade
practitioner of the poetical trade
striving to make his oracle heard
above the hissing of the absurd
looking on the masses with sardonic smile
inviolate in his inner self-exile
bidding loutish latter-day Horsemen pass by
with cold satirical and bloodshot eye
doing daily battle with the mental life
trying to forget he has a wife
padding about downstairs in curlers and slippers
endlessly embroiled in baked beans and kippers
as he meanwhile fumes and waits for the Holy Ghost
up there in his lonely observation post
a garret by chance carpeted and centrally heated
ensconced in armchair with pipe and pouch seated
the Sensitive Planted so beloved of Shelley
scaling Parnassus on well-nourished belly
with aesthetic energies to spend and burn
reaching at Fate's every barbarous turn
for bare bodkin or draught of swift hemlock
and finding the Jack Daniels still in stock.

Haunted hypochondriac and scholarly rake
steeped in the rustic lore of Clare and Blake
again excavating those satanic mills
in quest of metaphysical thrills
tireless indomitable intrepid wordsmith
daily living his secret beloved myth
that alone makes his life endurable
and his sanity almost insurable

preferring those Dantesque abysses
to the prattlings of the missus
that nymph of kippers and baked beans
slouching through Arcady in scruffy jeans
bringing him ham rolls and chicken soup
ministering to the marauding troop
of merest gut-need and appetite
unaware of his poetic pain and plight
poor painted heavy-hoofed Diana of the kitchen
mouthing endearments quite unbewitching
unknowing object of his private derision
oscillating between radio and television
blithe and trite and blissfully unheeding
as over typewriter her Percy Bysshe lies bleeding
thrashing in throes of latest ode or sonnet
pinning his transcendental soul upon it
while in the steamy nether regions downstairs
his lass of the most indelicate airs
lights up her umpteenth fag of that morning
and screams several shrill octaves without warning
for him to come down and show his husbandly mettle
by fixing the bloody plug on her electric kettle . . .

O though the world may never know it
he is every seedy inch a poet
as in clouds of fancy he sits alone
hugging the soul he thinks is his own.

Past Portrait

I sat for my friend the artist during a dull week
daring him to find me with his deft chalky strokes
drinking straight vodka and jabbering bright rubbish
never guessing he would unearth what he did
discover that which lay gnarled and hidden
beneath elaborate mounds of mimicry
and nudge it into such livid truth
no mirror could ever give back
finally leaving me wordless though glaring
confronting a stranger I knew darkly well
and wished not ever to know in light
vodka no longer victorious over visions
dredged up from depths I thought invulnerable
down years of diligent burial of things
that hindered cosy fantasies of self
held in a hollow shrine of careful conceit.

Yet there was fire then
the beginning of a voyage
anchored in proud solitudes
a surly arrogance almost noble
looking out at the woeful mess of a world
as if it owed me all the missing lore of life
and I would storm right out of time and claim it.

Four years on I stare at the face
a stranger I know not now in light or dark
and can discern but cannot feel the fire
nor remember the route of the journey
that floundered midway to nowhere
betrayed by an accident of truth.

Morning Song

Morning is where you move.

The strengthening sun
strokes the languid waves
gulls in a lazy ballet
perform miracles in still air
no longer wailing with need
as if they too were replete
with promise lyrical on the wind.

Islands half hid in mist
move soft against the sky
smoke upon burnt glass
mountains conversing with clouds
too early in their splendour to intimidate
with familiar awe of alien homecoming.

I grope about for words
to capture the morning
as a bird in song on a clifftop branch
reminds me of my puny arrogance
with no note of mockery in its voice
knowing the true artist between us.

Without need of words
aureoling my world
you smile at my frantic pace
to express the inexpressible
harbouring my small despairs
keeping me new for wonder
cradling my song.

Morning is where you move
and love-lucid my senses follow.

Constancy

The shadow lingers
of our separate yesterdays
blurring with menace our present light
casting the false aura of other ancient ardours
between the bright tenacious passion that binds us
unbreakable now and for the unguessable future.

There are no more subtle ways I can speak to you
save in halting verse like now
begging your charity.

Often lost with futile freedom in a wilderness
or more stranded still with frailer freedom in a cage;
this then is our latter-day choice.

More remote than star is from star
likewise are we sometimes in a room
each captive of our ghosts
stretching silences once treasured
beyond the faint felicity of touch
a cold place between us
no words can fill.

Hope and great danger hover
in our merest response
yet however tenuous our tomorrow
the truth remains:
Love is by far
more constant than lovers are.

Between the uncertainty and the dream
persists always the possibility of failure;
between the hopeless tenderness
and the unutterable dread
the knife-twist of rational resignation
to what neither of us condones in the other.

Our every day burgeons with promise or threat
still between the endearment and the curse
Love remains by far
more constant than lovers are.

The shadow lingers
blunting our clearer perceptions
of the true and lasting in each other
making all the more foredoomed the escape
into lucid articulate latitudes
in either wilderness or cage.

And more than a shadow's journey from the other
is immensely more than we can contemplate
since Love remains by far
more constant than lovers are.

Hope and a gradual peace
to inform our understanding
is my prayer for the unreadable future;
the better times are not easily put aside
and the underrated things in our life
speak with greater gentler command
than passing wrath.

We lose each other in ways wilful and insignificant
yet Love remains by far
more constant than ever lovers are.

Sour Note On A Sweet Ending

When I yield to the ultimate folly and die
– O in the vast unforeseeable by-and-by! –
promise me dearest you will send
no plastic roses at the end
shed no inordinate tears
nor harbour any nagging fears
that after I am safely gone
I will desecrate your dawn
with ghostly disquiet or confusion
to shatter your fond illusion
that you really are quite free of me
for the rest of your mortality.

In death as never once in life
as safe remove from temporal strife
as if good breeding with the worms began
I shall become quite the gentleman
and like an ever perfect host
preserve you from my inquisitive ghost
and from that unseemly flood of language
that had caused you such dire earthly anguish
and surely you will smile to see
how solicitous and pleasant I can be
how uncommonly courteous and brave
from the unquerulous side of the grave
though you will perhaps brush tear from eye
and aspirate a wondering sigh
that such a weight of words should be
gone clean into the earth with me
with barely a tremor left behind
to aggravate your unmarried mind –
hardly more than a publisher's blurb
to vexate and momentarily perturb
the new-found rhythm of your days
and you at length free of my boorish ways

a philosophical drink by your side
alone in the companionable eventide
with me not there to plunder your peace
with unstoppable garbage without cease
while silently suffering you lift glass or cup
and mutely implore me to belt bloody up . . .

Ah dearest heart if you will but wait
I'll become the ideal soulmate
nevermore causing you a moment's trouble
and I but a mere ectoplasmic bubble
swaying above your gorgeous head
gruff and garrulous and safely dead.

A Blunt Instrument

Is my muse
a wild boar blundering blind
through delicate stems of themes
leaving a gory mess of butchered images
in its plundering wilful wake?

Maddened by murderous interior music
it ravages sunsets
captured once only by Turner
smears dark slivers of blood
across the face of the clearest moon;
the serenest swan static in majesty
upon evening waters
recoils from it in panic
and singing birds at its approach
drop like stones down the sky.

A thing of remorseless gluttony
of immense invincible vacuity
is my muse.

Yet it sang once in a rare moment
a small pure indomitable sound
escaping from twisted strings
and somehow after that
I could almost love the grotesque creature
as one can sometimes come to love the misbegotten.

Billy Nowhere

In smaller kinder places
where tongues are slow to taunt
and minds keep pace with turning leaves
he would have been acclaimed the village idiot
crowned with spiky laurels of honest wit and no malice
as something peculiar unto the wind
a few slates missing upstairs to be sure
but harmless and daft as a jackrabbit
dodging a friendly fusillade of potshots
aimed only to make him jump and never to maim.

In our deadlier clime no such mercies abounded.

We called him Billy Nowhere
for nowhere he seemed to be going
save up and down the murderous maze of roads
sweeping up the endless debris of other people's lives
falling into sudden profound reveries in the midst of dust.

O jealous we were of this readymade Quasimodo
streetcorner Caesars spawned in sewer depths of intent
hissing forth precocious maledictions to outwit serpents
aroused to young green bile by his intolerable innocence
jerking to the ragged rhythm of our spiteful mocking bells
clanging after him as he swept up rivulets of filth
banning him from our games of cocksure daring
forever devising new schemes of pointless pain
to rub his twisted nose in the gutters
the City Fathers hired him to clean
in all his twenty-very-odd years
of bovine boyhood enraging us
pale eggshell eyes puzzled
and a weak cunning grin opening to our queries
as we asked him what colour knickers
his sister wore at her shotgun wedding

and "None!" he cannily replied
knowing it would please us.

Leaning on his massive yardbrush in the watery morning
dustclouds gathering about his splayed hobnailed feet
his few thoughts creeping up and down his face
timid as mice uncertain of the light
trying to make out the mystery of our malice
sighing and wetting his horned hands with a manly spit
the better to get on with his streetcleaning destiny
shuffling off into the ineffectual sunset
his oxen hours nearing tired finale.

Later when he grew less "simple"
he would cadge pints off us in smoky bars
jabbering out the latest pop tunes
in a brownish spray of saliva
slobbering like a dog promised goodies
fawning upon our grownup snarled obscenities
the abbreviated ancient weekend suit hanging on his bones
in ragged parody of staunch hardihood
and at our braggart prompting he would follow
married women home at closing time
as far as their lighted windows
before flinging himself with manic glee
into the dewy midnight bushes above their shrill curses.

For all I know of him now in my crabbed nowhere decades
he is still sweeping the same blind streets
hounded by new hordes of devil children
his wrinkled monkey face dusty and undefeated.

Lost Lullaby

Where oh where has my innocence gone
where oh where can it be?
I mislaid it some years ago I recall
in a house of cheap love on the quay.

Where oh where has my innocence gone
where oh where can it be?
It dissolved in tears of petty rage
when the world refused to praise me.

Where oh where has my innocence gone
where oh where can it be?
It fled when the friend I trusted most
played the fool and began to trust me.

Where oh where has my innocence gone
where oh where can it be?
I lost it the day my heart became wise
and refused to return to me.

My innocence fled and took away
the key to my prison soul
leaving no star to falter by
and no crumbs for my beggar bowl.

It will not come back again
however my promise beguiled
until the man forgets his foolish estate
and greets the world as a child.

Oriental

How sad
To be alone in Taipeh
sipping Rose's lime juice
knowing your favourite lotus flower
lies tonight with a lesser envoy
from a country not mentioned
in the best circles.
Thinking how the coming nights
will be so many dyspeptic yawns without her,
recalling as you clean your teeth
the tumult of her sapling thighs
catapulting you into heavens beyond count
recalling her soft giggling vowels
against your stifled mouth
in the month of the long moon
in the cool white room of remote charm
facing China.

How sad
standing on the filthy railway station
brown briefcase in hand
pig eyes lost behind thick lenses
waving farewell to your boss the ambassador
who that night will resume undiplomatic relations
with his wife of the varicose-veined legs
and daunting Everest bosom;
thoughts snap at you like gnats
provoking a mild despair
and quietly you cry into yourself
recalling the empty room back at the embassy
her imprint everywhere, the sheets and pillows,
the Axminster carpet, in the scented bathroom
airy with lotus blossoms climbing the walls.
Tonight there will be no sleep in the room facing China,
thinking of her crushed like silk

under the lesser envoy;
perhaps you will then at last think of your wife
back home in bed in Westchester County
state of New York
snuggling down with caramels and Steinbeck.

How sad
alone in Taipeh
sipping Rose's lime juice
waiting to go mad
hearing the mocking laughter begin
of hidden perfumed harlots who will taunt without let
in the dog-eaten months of the long and short moon
facing China.

Slug Song

Consider the ubiquitous slug
be it snail, termite or bug
asking nothing save stalk or leaf
quite untroubled by metaphysic belief
inhabiting palaces of rock and river
sliding through life with sinuous quiver
minute lord of the plenteous earth
devouring it for all its diluvial worth.

By man's inveterate wrath subjected
to man's vast follies it stays unaffected
and I note yet another instance of its sagacity
wriggling along with such admirable tenacity;
however long it may have dawdled and tarried
I have yet to hear of a slug getting married
while I sit surrounded by manifold reminders
of what should have been eye-opening blinders
of what man's foolhardy supercilious estate
has wreaked on that most singular state
as I sadly contemplate my own crass contributions
to that enriching pluperfect of institutions.

And O joyous excellence of the humble slug –
it meanders through time without need of drug
crawling with sedate resolve to its destiny
undulating with serpentine zest and assiduity
and what matter if it fails to deduct or think –
certain it is that the slug does not drink
for who ever heard of bug, termite or worm
no matter how madly they shiver and squirm
in all manner of primordial esoteric dances
going into silly transcendental trances?

O how I envy snail, termite and slug
snug as God willed it in the proverbial rug
all petty guile lacking and unassuming
never once knowing what it is to be human.

A Question For Myself

Letters of hangdog devotion
moist with fatuous nostalgia
trickling in from your past
every other month or so
from a person now stateless in your realm

strike me as both ridiculous and sad
as though watching a cripple on crutches
buoyed up by invincible optimism
trying to cross a crowded thoroughfare
to catch the last bus
that left ages ago.

It's a form of obscenity
this burrowing back into the past
such ardent archaeology of dead stones
never letting the relics abide in peace
never allowing the past to be decently dead.

I' too am invincible in my optimism
cocksure you won't throw him a spar
or help him across the busy street
that now like a vast prayer divides you
cocooned in my snug assurance
knowing it is with me you'll be watching
the rise and fall of every new and old moon
from this blessed day on to the inconceivable end.

Round every corner of mind and eye
you are there to startle with newest joy
my glimmering world entwined upon your word.

Why then am I so bloody afraid?

In Absentia

Scrounging solace from scraps of remembered talk
                 I wander about the bleak November house
                       from room to eyeless room
my mind plucking at fragments
                    at images that would hold it
                  back from the final zero plunge
knowing the absurdity of my misery
                     knowing you will be back
                but in the small infinities before noon
night is a receding promise.

I search in these vacant hours
                 when flowers are dying
                  for small familiar distractions
in printed word and pictured page
                  in the well-loved antics of our
animals
       and find only a keener melancholy
               knowing they grieve in your absence too
               without tongue to put to it.

Scrounging broken scraps of solace
                 from room to heartless room
a disgruntled disinherited ghost
                I observe the jaded grass
                  below my window
dry and brittle as hope gone sour
                 a lone sparrow talking to itself
                  on a dead branch.

Dark and there will come the swish and glide of wheels
                     on wet gravel
                     doors opening and
shutting

                        your step and voice in the kitchen
                                    the dogs frantic in welcome
the more sedate greeting of the cat
                                    curling herself round your
insteps.

You will be tired
                        but you will smile and touch my hair
                                    and ask me how I spent *my* day
and not being brave I will tell you.

We will laugh and have a few slow drinks by the fire
                        and in the night next to you
                                    most near as my own lulled flesh
I will be tortured by a dream of you
                                    never coming back.

Visitors

Soft upon a whispered adieu
the moonlit visitors sail out
jewelled with remembrance
upon their bright coffin slabs
out of sight and never out of mind
behind the silver lisp of faint shore voices
burning forever in singing stones

A look spearing folded leaves
fragile brush of fingertips
ineffable and certain as the wind
a dialogue the shuttered brain cannot snare
and a star hisses headlong to earth
trailing immemorial airs
as footfalls die

A cloud stirs upon the moon
a slow sure wink
and fragrant waves below
inform the night with peace

In my room of midnight rhymes
the loud busy chat of the fire
the book spread sacrificial upon the table
I inhabit again the old cosy dimensions
and ponder on the new friends I have made
in all the mute moonlit eloquence of death
telling me this place is mine and theirs

and the shadows will ever be kind to me.

Old Lady

Miss Mahaffey was her name
all faded lace and silver hair
her face already a skull upon the pillow
lit eerily at night from the streetlight
beaming at the mouth of the narrow lane
below the dull distempered walls of her ward

a frail rainbow fall of silk
faintly smudged at the edges
was little Miss Mahaffey
shrunken and sunken into yesterday
fragile shadow on parched landscape
fingers stirring like limp mice
twitching on the winding shrouds of sheets
maiden lady clinging to grace and dignity
gently lying in her perpetual twilight
not bothering the hurrying nurses for a drop of water
brought by life's meaner barbarities to this
wrinkled and shrivelled up in a crisp bed
coughing up phlegm and speckled blood
being incontinent in the night

a genteel ghost whispering words of no complaint
patient as the plot of earth marked out
to receive her few fish-thin bones
all beauty safely behind her
save briefly when she opened her eyes
to the night nurse bending over her
and murmured "sorry".

Harlequinade

Out of the dark
into a place of song
night a concourse of bright tongues
light outwitting the stars
in galaxies of required glamour

Hear behind the talk
rising behind the tinkle of raised glass
a small cry of need
a cry from the maimed
the forgotten and dispossessed
in whose behalf now
this banquet of no charity is laid
and the nightlong dance begins

Contemplate without malice
from a subtle distance without
this rainbow bowl
of festooned fishes
elegant or estranged
in their respective ecstasies
eddying in perplexed parables of pleasure
engaged in a louder charade
than the one below the surface
muted in patient régimes of pain

Long may the harlequinade spin out
if it takes us away from the tumbrel.